KT-555-929

Sunshine

Joy Palmer

Watts Books
London • New York • Sydney

© 1992 Franklin Watts
This edition 1995

Watts Books
96 Leonard Street
London EC2A 4RH

Franklin Watts Australia
14 Mars Road
Lane Cove
NSW 2066

UK ISBN: 0 7496 0645 2

Series editor: A. Patricia Sechi
Design: Shaun Barlow
Cover design: Edward Kinsey
Artwork: Karen Johnson
Cover artwork: Hugh Dixon
Picture research: Ambreen Husain

A CIP catalogue record for this book
is available from the British Library

Printed in Italy by G. Canale & C. SpA

King's Road Primary School
Rosyth - Tel: 313470

Contents

What is sunshine?

The earth's heat and light comes from the sun. Rays of sunlight shine on our planet as it moves around in space. Sunshine is energy. It is produced by the sun, a huge **sphere** of heat and light at the centre of our **solar system**. Without the sun's energy, there would be no light or life on earth.

▽ There is life on earth, thanks to the light and warmth of the sun.

Hot and cold

Some places on earth receive less heat and light from the sun than others. The sun's rays must travel further to reach the north and south poles. Here, the curve of the earth makes the sun's rays spread out over a larger area of the earth's surface. As a result, these areas are colder than those at the **equator**. The hottest places on earth are around the equator.

▷ The sun's rays are very weak at the poles. The air still feels cold.

▽ The sun's rays travel in straight lines. They are at their strongest at the equator. At the poles, the rays are spread over a larger area of the earth's surface and feel cooler.

Journey around the sun

The earth continually circles around the sun. It takes a year to go round it once. As the earth moves, it always tilts in the same direction. The part of the earth tilting towards the sun receives more sunlight. There it is summer. On the part of the earth tilting away from the sun it is winter. As the earth moves around the sun, the seasons of the year change.

▽ The earth tilts to one side. For a few months of the year, the north is nearer to the sun than the south. As the earth moves around the sun, this changes. The south moves nearer to the sun.

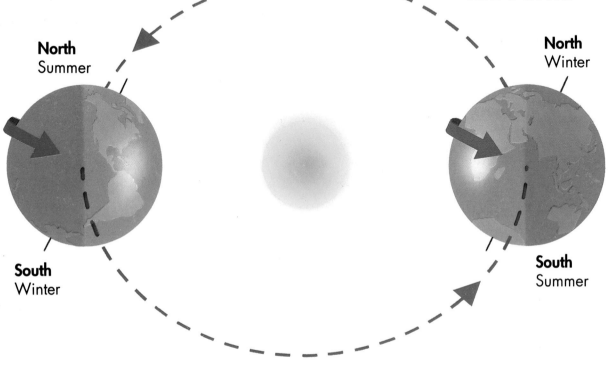

North
Summer

North
Winter

South
Winter

South
Summer

Seasons change as
the earth tilts
towards or away
from the sun.

Sun for life

All living things depend on the sun's rays. Without sun there would be no grass, trees or flowers. Green plants could not survive without sunshine. Their leaves use sunlight to help make food for the whole plant. This process is called **photosynthesis.** Without plants, animals and people would have no food to eat.

▽ Plants need sunlight for healthy growth. They will always grow towards the light. Green plants use sunlight to make food.

▷ In the light, a potato will grow fat, healthy shoots. In the dark, its shoots are pale and thin.

▽ Sunshine enables crops to grow and ripen, providing food for people and animals.

Heat from space

The sun is about 93 million miles away from the earth. Its light rays take about $8\frac{1}{2}$ minutes to reach us. They filter through the **atmosphere** before reaching the earth's surface. The atmosphere acts like a blanket keeping in the warmth of the sun. A layer of gas in the atmosphere, called the **ozone layer,** blocks out the sun's harmful rays. Recently, pollution on earth has started attacking the ozone layer and making holes in it.

▽ The ozone layer acts like a shield. It reflects the sun's harmful rays.

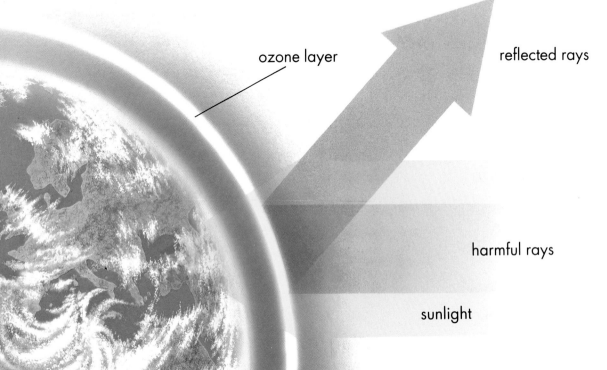

ozone layer

reflected rays

harmful rays

sunlight

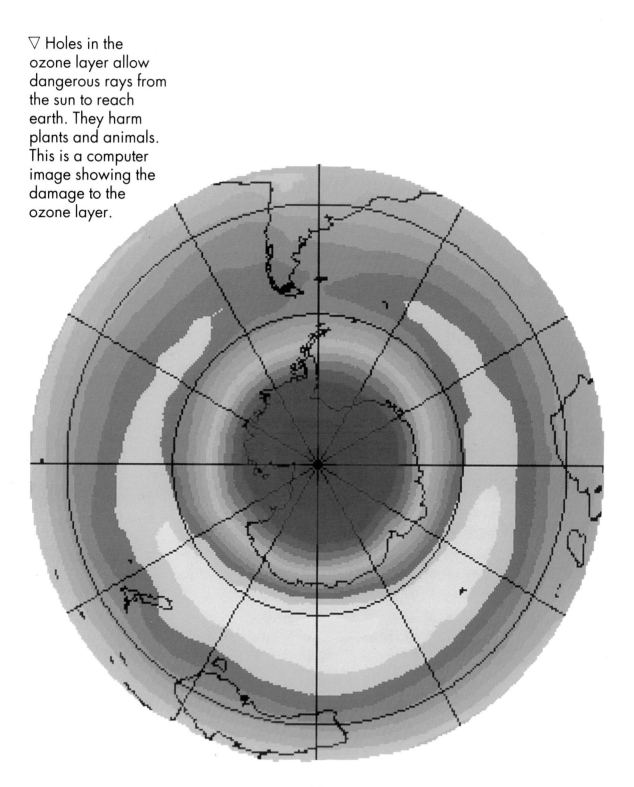

▽ Holes in the ozone layer allow dangerous rays from the sun to reach earth. They harm plants and animals. This is a computer image showing the damage to the ozone layer.

Measuring sunshine

People who study the weather are called **meteorologists.** A special instrument is used to measure the number of hours of sunshine each day. A glass ball **reflects** light rays from the sun on to a piece of card. This light is so warm that it burns a mark on the card. The mark tells us how many hours of sunshine there were during the day.

▷ Light clothing helps to keep you cool on a hot, sunny day. How else can you keep cool?

▽ This instrument is used to measure sunshine. The sun's rays bounce off a glass ball and burn a mark on the paper.

▽ We use a thermometer to measure the temperature of the air. The thermometer should be placed in the shade, not in the sun.

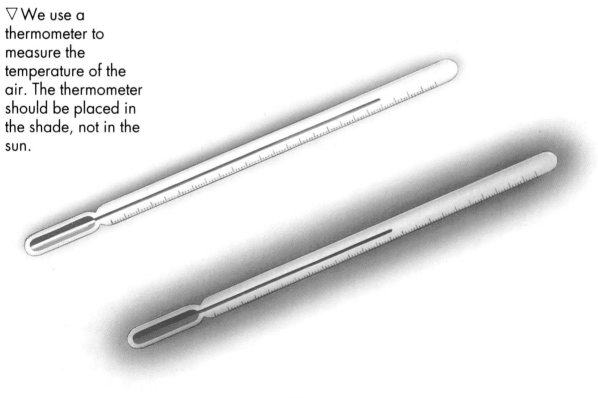

Using the sun

We use the sun's heat and light in many ways. Some of the earliest clocks used sunlight to tell the time. The first sundials were invented thousands of years ago. They relied on the length and position of shadows cast by objects in the sun.

Heat from the sun's rays causes water to **evaporate.** People all over the world use the sun to dry clothes, fish, fruit and other crops.

▷ Dried food keeps longer. When these grapes are dry, they will be packaged and sold as raisins.

▽ Water evaporates in the warmth of the sun. As seawater evaporates, it leaves behind salt which we use for cooking.

▽ You can tell the time on a sundial by watching the length and position of the shadow cast by the sun.

People in the sun

People who live near to the equator at the centre of the earth are used to very hot, sunny weather. The sun's rays shine directly on to the lands where they live. Different ways have been discovered or invented to cope with the heat. Some modern homes have air conditioning. Others might have small windows and thick white walls. People also wear loose, light clothing to help them keep cool.

▽ In hot countries, many houses are painted white to help keep out the sun. Hats and light clothing keep people cool.

▷ Modern inventions, such as refrigerators, keep food fresh for longer in the hottest weather.

▽ Blinds and umbrellas provide shade when it's too hot to sit in the sun.

Animals and the sun

When the sun is very hot, animals and birds find ways of keeping cool. Bushes and rocks provide useful shelter. Some creatures burrow beneath the surface of the ground to the cooler layers below. Many insects, such as bees and butterflies, become active in the sun. Dragonflies hover over ponds in the warm air.

▷ Some birds fly thousands of kilometres during the year to find warm, sunny weather. This is called migration.

▷ Insects need the sun to become active. They feed on summer flowers.

18

▽ Air blowing across a rabbit's ears cools the animal on a hot day.

△ Lizards and snakes bask in the warm sun. They may take shelter or burrow in the sand if it gets too hot.

Plants and the sun

All green plants need sunlight to make their own food. Plants take in water from the soil which then evaporates through the leaves. The bigger the leaf, the more water is lost. Some plants can store water in their stems and are able to survive in hot, dry surroundings. Their leaves are usually small and tough.

▷ Sunflowers turn their heads to follow the sun in the sky. Their seeds ripen in the warm sun.

▽ Cereals need plenty of sunshine to help them grow and ripen.

◁ The agave plant grows in hot, dry places. It stores water inside its tough leaves. Sharp spines protect it from thirsty animals.

Power from the sun

The sun's energy, or **solar energy,** can be used to heat buildings, and provide hot water. Solar panels are used to collect the sun's heat. In sunny countries, many homes and their water supplies can be heated this way. The light of the sun can also be used to produce electricity. This is a very valuable source of power because it will not run out like other fuels.

▽ This furnace in the South of France is powered by solar energy. Reflectors turn the solar energy into electricity, even when the sun is behind the clouds.

◁ The sun shines on solar panels on the roof of a house. The sun's energy can be used to heat water.

▽ Solar-powered freezers are a good choice for hot countries. They are used by the Red Cross to store medicines.

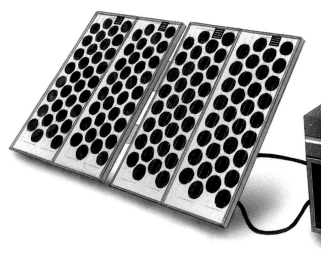

△ Some pocket calculators run on sunlight which they store in solar cells.

Heatwave

Sunshine can be very unpredictable. Some of our summers are much warmer than others. From time to time, there may be a heatwave when hot, dry, sunny weather lasts for many weeks. This can cause problems. Soil becomes hard and dry, and crops do not grow. There may be a serious water shortage. The hot sun causes water in ponds and streams to evaporate, leaving wildlife with no water.

▷ Animals that live in water may die when rivers and streams dry up.

▽ Crops do not thrive in hot, dry weather. The harvest may fail.

▽ In hot, dry spells people may have their water cut off, and have to use standpipes in the street.

▽ In a dry summer, water may be short. People are not allowed to use hosepipes to fill pools or wash their cars.

Keeping ourselves protected

Too much sun can harm people. People who live in hot, **tropical** lands have dark skin which shields them from the sun. Their skin has a good supply of melanin. This helps protect them from the harmful rays of the sun. Fair-skinned people do not have as much melanin. They need to take care in the sun. It can be very bad to sit in the sun's direct light for too long.

▷ Melanin helps to protect our skin in the sun. Everybody has some melanin in their skin. People with darker skins have more.

▽ One way to protect your skin from the sun is to cover up with a hat and light clothing.

▽ You need suncreams, sunglasses and plenty of drinks during a day in the sun.

Enjoying the sun

People who live in countries with cold winters look forward to warm summers. People spend more time outside in the sunshine – cooking and eating outdoors, playing games and listening to music, as well as swimming and other sports. As long as you are well protected, it is good to feel the warmth of the sun on your skin.

▷ Many people enjoy open-air concerts on warm summer evenings.

▽ It can be good fun cooking a meal on a barbeque and eating outside. An umbrella gives shade if the sun gets too hot.

△ Another way to
enjoy a sunny day is
to go swimming and
play on the beach.

29

Things to do

- To make a sundial, fix a pencil into a ball of plasticine on a piece of stiff card. Place it in a sunny place on the ground or on top of a wall. Draw a line along the shadow made by the pencil. Write the correct time at the end of the shadow. Do this every hour through the day. Note when the shadows are longest and shortest.

- Sunlight contains seven different colours. To see them you will need:
    - a small mirror
    - a piece of white card
    - a small tray of water.

Put the tray in a sunny place opposite the white card. Hold the mirror at one side of the tray so that the sunlight shines onto the mirror. Move the mirror about until you can see rainbow colours on the card.

Glossary

atmosphere A thick layer of air that surrounds the earth.

bask To lie in the sun.

equator An imaginary line around the middle of the earth.

evaporate To change from a liquid into a gas. When water evaporates, it changes into invisible droplets in the air called water vapour.

meteorologist Someone who studies, measures and forecasts the weather.

ozone layer A layer of gas in the atmosphere. It protects earth from the sun's harmful rays.

photosynthesis The way that green plants make their own food, using sunlight, water and part of the air.

reflect To throw back heat or light.

solar energy The power of sunlight which can be used to work or drive machines.

solar system The sun, together with the planets going round it. In our solar system there are nine planets.

sphere A round, ball-shaped body in space. Planets, moons and the sun are all spheres.

tropical In a place near the equator, on either side of it.

31

Index

King's Road Primary School
Rosyth - Tel: 313470

Picture credits: Bruce Coleman
Ltd (J Shaw) 3, (J Murray) 13,
(M Freeman) 17; Chris
Fairclough Colour Library 27;
Frank Lane Picture Library
(L Batten) 25; Robert Harding
(G Renner) 5, (F Costello) 15;
Science Photo Library (NASA)
11, (T Craddock) 22; Swift
Picture Library (M King) 19;
ZEFA 9, 21, 29.